P9-AOV-102

Small Plays for You and a Friend

by SUE ALEXANDER

Pictures by OLIVIA H. H. COLE

A Clarion Book
THE SEABURY PRESS
New York

For my children Glenn, Marc, and Stacey . . .
especially Stacey who asked for this book

Text copyright © 1973 by Sue Alexander.
Illustrations copyright © 1973 by Scholastic Magazines, Inc.

This edition is published by The Seabury Press, Inc.,
by arrangement with Scholastic Book Services, a division
of Scholastic Magazines, Inc.

Library of Congress Cataloging in Publication Data

Alexander, Sue.
    Small plays for you and a friend.

    SUMMARY: Five original plays designed for two
actors, with the author's notes on staging and adapting
the plays, including simple directions for the actors
and a list of the props needed.
    [1. Plays] I. Cole, Olivia H. H., illus.
II. Title.
PN6120.A5A39   812'.5'4   74-4019
ISBN 0-8164-3125-6

A note about this book

You and a friend can act out the five plays in this book all by yourselves. There are two characters in each play. Most of the characters can be played by either a girl or a boy.

It is fun to do the plays over and over. You and your friend can take turns playing the different parts.

At the beginning of each play, you will see a list of things you need when you put on the play. You will find most of them right in your house. If you do not have some of the things, think of other things that would work just as well.

Don't worry about costumes. You can do the plays in your everyday clothes—it's just as much fun.

You and your friend may want to put on two or three of these plays in a special show for your family and friends, or for your class. Maybe you will make up more small plays of your own.

How to read the plays:

The words in color are the words you say.
The words in black tell you what to do.

What's in My Soup?

But look! There's a snail in my soup!

And it isn't even snail soup!

5

Characters in this play

A waiter (or a waitress)

A customer

MENU

6

Things you will need:

A table and a chair

A soup bowl and a spoon

A piece of cardboard folded to make a menu

A small pad of paper and a pencil

A towel to put over the waiter's arm,
or an apron

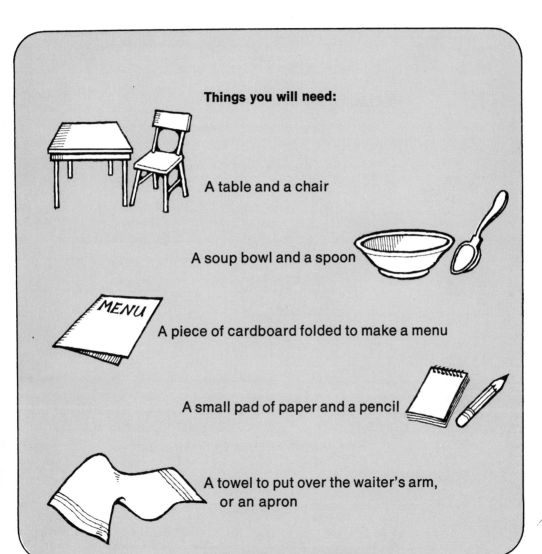

7

The play begins:

The customer walks to the table and sits down in the chair.

The waiter comes in with a menu and a pad of paper and pencil.

The waiter hands the menu to the customer.

WAITER: May I take your order?

The customer looks at menu carefully.

CUSTOMER: Let me see. I think I will have some soup.

WAITER: **Certainly.**

He writes the order on the pad and goes out.

The waiter comes back with a bowl and a spoon.

Here you are.

The waiter sets the bowl and spoon on the table in front of the customer.

The customer looks into the bowl.

CUSTOMER: **There is a fly in my soup!**

WAITER: Oh my! Let me get you a fresh bowl.

The waiter takes the bowl away.

Then he comes back with the bowl and sets it down on the table.

Here is some more soup. I hope it is all right.

The customer looks into the bowl.

CUSTOMER: Well, there isn't any fly. But look! There's a snail in my soup!

WAITER: **And it isn't even snail soup!
I'll get you some more.**

The waiter takes the bowl away.

Then he brings it back.

I hope *this* one is all right.

11

CUSTOMER: **Well, there isn't any fly and there isn't any snail . . . but look! There is a SNAKE in my soup!**

The customer gets up and jumps away from the table.

I'm not going to eat here! I'm going to go to the other restaurant on the corner!

WAITER: I don't blame you! Wait, I'll go with you!

He throws his towel on the table and they run off together.

Zabba, Zabba, Zoom!

Oh no! That will make me melt!

13

Characters in this play

A witch (or a wizard)

A traveler

14

Things you will need:

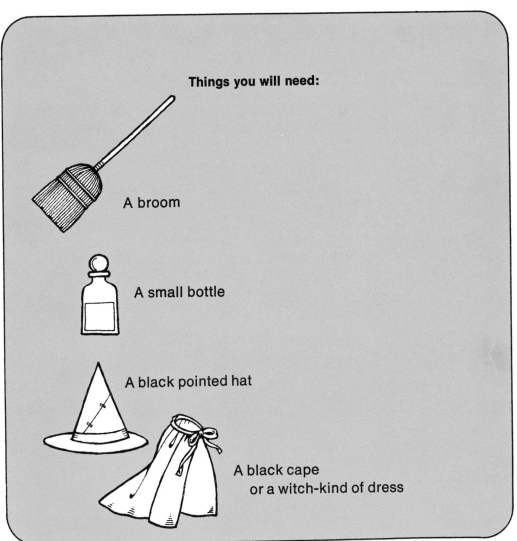

A broom

A small bottle

A black pointed hat

A black cape
or a witch-kind of dress

15

The play begins:

A broom is lying on the ground in the forest.
A small bottle is near it.

The traveler comes walking along. She trips over the broom.

TRAVELER: What a funny place to find a broom!

She picks it up.

Who would ever think a broom would be lying here in the middle of the forest?

16

The witch runs in.

WITCH: Don't touch my broom! Don't touch my broom!

She grabs the broom out of the traveler's hands.

Who are you? And what are you doing in my forest?

TRAVELER: I'm just traveling through. I didn't know it was your broom . . . or your forest.

WITCH: It is! It is!

She stamps her foot on the ground.

You don't belong here!
I am going to change you into a duck!

The witch points her finger at the traveler.

WITCH: ZABBA, ZABBA, ZOOM!

The traveler begins to walk like a duck.

TRAVELER: Quack, quack! Quack, quack!

WITCH: That's too noisy.
I'll change you into a frog.

She points her finger at the traveler.

ZABBA, ZABBA, ZOOM!

The traveler begins to hop around like a frog.

TRAVELER: **Croak! Croak! Croak!**

WITCH: **That won't do either. Let me see. What else can I change you into? I know! A monkey! ZABBA, ZABBA, ZOOM!**

The traveler dances around like a monkey.

She sees the small bottle on the ground.

She dances over to it and picks it up.

WITCH: **Oh no! Not that.**

The witch looks very frightened. She starts to back away.

The traveler looks at the bottle and then at the witch.

Then she starts to chase the witch.

Oh no! That will make me melt! Keep away!

The traveler catches up to the witch and turns the bottle upside down over her head.

WITCH: I'm melting! I'm melting!

TRAVELER: And I'm turning back into myself!

WITCH: Ohhhhhhhhh . . .

The witch falls down in a heap.

TRAVELER: **Well, that settles that. I can take what is left of the mean old witch and throw her into the trash.**

She picks up the broom and sweeps the witch out.

The Frog Princess

Oh! Who are you? And how did you get here?

SPRINKLE ME

23

Characters in this play

A man

A princess who has been turned into a frog

24

Things you will need:

A small bottle

A sign with the words "Sprinkle Me"

SPRINKLE ME

A large piece of green material, such as a green sheet or blanket

A princess-kind of dress

A man's shirt and tie

if you want to dress up

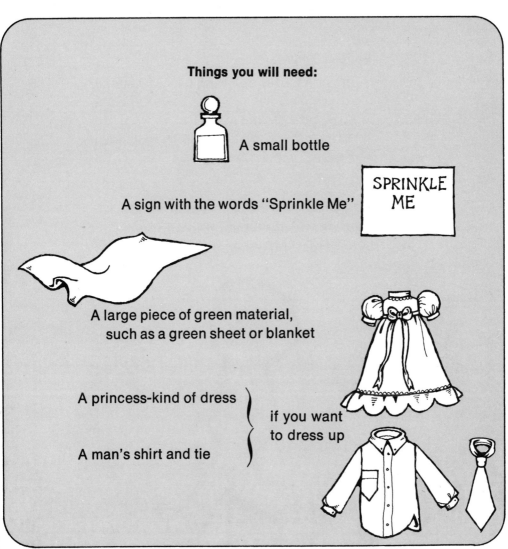

25

The play begins:

The princess is sitting all tucked up under the green material. (She has been turned into a frog by a wicked witch.)

On the ground next to her is the small bottle with the "Sprinkle Me" sign.

A man comes walking along.

MAN: It's a long way through these woods. I wonder if I shall ever find a friend to help me find my way out.

PRINCESS: **Croak! Croak!**

MAN: **What a big frog!**

PRINCESS: **Croak! Croak! Croak!**

The man walks around the frog — and he sees the bottle.

He picks it up.

MAN: **Hmmmmm. What is this funny bottle?
I wonder who put it here.**

PRINCESS: **Croak! Croak!**

MAN: **And what is this sign? It says "Sprinkle Me."**

The man opens the bottle and turns it upside down. He shakes it.

PRINCESS (as loud as she can): **CROAK! CROAK! CROAK!**

MAN: **What a noisy frog. Maybe if I sprinkle some of this stuff on him, he will be quiet.**

He sprinkles the frog.

The princess throws off the green cover and stands up.

MAN: Oh! Who are you? And how did you get here?

PRINCESS I am Princess Rose Anne.
The wicked witch turned me into a frog.
You found the magic sprinkles that turned me
back into a princess again.
Thank you! Thank you!
Is there any way I can help you now?

MAN: **Yes. Be my friend and show me how to get out of these woods.**

PRINCESS: **I'd be glad to.**

The princess and the man go off together.

Hello, Little Dog

Bow-wow! Ruff!

Oh, little dog that's the best trick of all!

31

Characters in this play

A child

A little dog

Things you will need:

A book

A folded newspaper

A short piece of rope to be used as the dog's tail

33

The play begins:

The child is walking home from school with a book in her hand.

The little dog (on hands and knees) comes up, wagging his tail.

LITTLE DOG: **Bow-wow! Bow-wow!**

CHILD: **Hello, little dog. I've never seen you before. Where did you come from?**

LITTLE DOG: **Bow-wow! Ruff!**

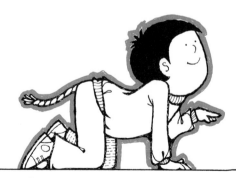

CHILD: **Well, I'm going home now. Don't follow me.
My mother doesn't like dogs.**

The little dog follows.

**I said don't follow me!
But you are really cute, little dog.
I wonder . . . no, I guess she wouldn't.**

LITTLE DOG: **Bow-wow! Ruff!**

He does a somersault.

CHILD: **That's a great trick! Can you do any more?**

The little dog sits up and begs.

CHILD: That's wonderful, little dog!
Can you do something else?
Can you give me your paw?

LITTLE DOG: Ruff!

He holds out his paw.

The child shakes hands with the dog.

CHILD: There never was a little dog as smart as you!

The child pats the dog on the head, then turns away sadly.

I just wish my mother liked dogs.

The child walks a little way with her head down.

The dog follows.

Suddenly the child stops.

CHILD: Oh dear, here is my house.
I will have to say good-bye, little dog.

The dog whimpers softly.

Then he sees a folded newspaper lying on the ground.

He becomes very excited.

LITTLE DOG: Bow-wow! Bow-wow! Ruff!

The dog runs over to the newspaper.

He picks it up in his mouth and brings it to the child.

The child takes the newspaper.

CHILD: Oh, little dog, that's the best trick of all!
I'm going to tell my mother how smart you are.
Then maybe, just maybe . . .
You wait here!

> The child runs off. A few seconds later, she comes back.
>
> She is very happy.
>
> She jumps up and down.

Guess what, little dog! Mother said I could keep you. Come on in!

> The little dog jumps around, wagging his tail.

LITTLE DOG: Ruff! Bow-wow! Ruff!

> He does one more somersault and goes off with the child.

Goom-bya, Room-bya, Zerko!

Wait, King! Give me another chance!

All right. But you had better do a good trick this time.

39

Characters in this play

A king (or a queen)

A magician

40

Things you will need:

A chair

A cape for the magician

A paper crown for the king or queen

A pot with a handkerchief in it

A penny

An old sheet

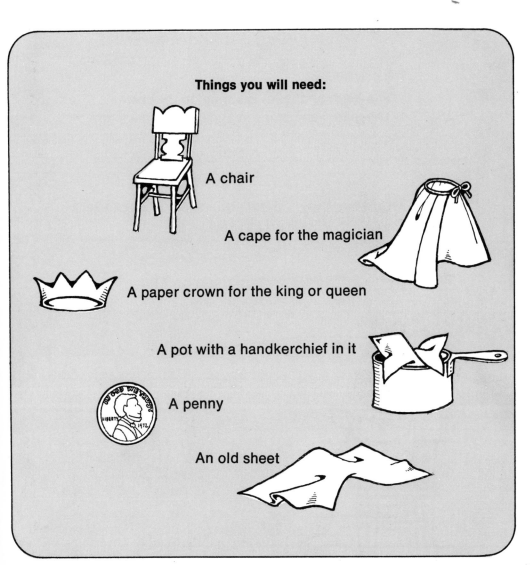

41

The play begins:

The king (or queen) is sitting on the chair.
The magician comes in and bows to the king.

KING: Magician, they tell me your name is Razzadazz the Great. What I want to know is . . . how *Great* are you?

MAGICIAN: I am a very good magician, King. I know lots of tricks.

KING: **Well, we shall see. But I must warn you —
I have a terrible temper. Now, do one
of your tricks for me.**

MAGICIAN: **All right.**

He goes out and comes back with a pot.

**I shall pull a rabbit out of this pot.
GOOM-BYA, ROOM-BYA, ZERKO!**

43

He waves his hand over the pot, then reaches in.

He pulls out a handkerchief.

MAGICIAN: Oh dear! I wonder what went wrong. Oh dear!

The king jumps out of the chair.

KING: Razzadazz, you are a TERRIBLE magician. I will send you away forever!

MAGICIAN: Wait, King! Give me another chance! I know more tricks.

KING: **Hmmmm.**

He sits down.

**All right. I will give you another chance.
But you had better do a good trick this time.**

MAGICIAN: **Oh, I will!**

He goes out and comes back with a penny.

King, I shall change this penny into a dollar!

He puts the penny in the handkerchief and
waves his hands around.

GOOM-BYA, ROOM-BYA, ZERKO!

Razzadazz opens the handkerchief.

The penny is still there.

The king jumps up again and shakes his fists.

KING: You are NOT a good magician! That is still a penny! Now I AM going to send you away forever!

MAGICIAN: Wait! Please wait! I know another trick. And it ALWAYS works!

KING: **Well, all right. I will give you just ONE more chance.**

The king sits down again.

The magician runs out and comes back with a sheet.

MAGICIAN: **For this trick, King, you will have to come close to me.**

The king gets off his chair and stands near Razzadazz.

KING: **Like this?**

MAGICIAN: **Closer!**

KING: **Now what?**

MAGICIAN: **Now I will make us both disappear!
GOOM-BYA, ROOM-BYA, ZERKO!**

He puts the sheet over both himself and
the king.

They go out together.

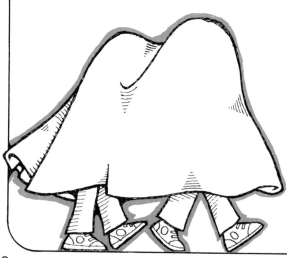